SOLD OUT IN FIFTEEN SECONDS

NFTs for Gaming, Art, Investments, Graffiti, and Digital Disneyland

Jamil Hasan

SOLD OUT IN FIFTEEN SECONDS

Table of Contents

Introducing the Crypto Hipster's Chronicles — 5

Chapter 1: How Graffiti Kings and Street Art are Capturing the NFT Art World's Attention and Trust — 9

Chapter 2: NFTs for Dummies — 31

Chapter 3: Stepping into the Metaverse: Building Digital Disneyland — 57

Chapter 4: Money Sports, Decentralized Gaming, and the Building of a Brand-New Industry — 79

Appendix A: About the Author — 105

Appendix B: Crypto Hipster Podcasts — 111

Appendix C: Crypto Hipster's Chronicles — 139

SOLD OUT IN FIFTEEN SECONDS

SOLD OUT IN FIFTEEN SECONDS

Introducing the Crypto Hipster's Chronicles

During my five plus years in the cryptocurrency, digital asset, and blockchain industry, I have accomplished a variety of things in the space, including authoring this book, my seventh book, with many more to come, and hosting over 190 podcasts. My Crypto Hipster Podcasts (anchor.fm/crypto-hipster-podcast) differ from post other cryptocurrency podcasts. While the top venture capital studios focused on price and market action of Bitcoin, alternative coins, NFTs and metaverses, I focused on something else:

The long-term societal and personal benefits of blockchain technology use cases, globally.

I then compiled three to five individual podcasts at a time to create Crypto Hipster's Chronicles. These compilations are more than just a catchy compilation. They all center around a common

SOLD OUT IN FIFTEEN SECONDS

theme, a theme based on "human" issues. These human issues include societal, mindset, social skills, and personal growth and development.

I have titled the eighth compilation for Crypto Hipster's Chronicles, Episode 8, "NFTs Arising from the Ashes", and that episode I have now converted into this book.

Coming out of COVID-19, the year 2021 started a renaissance movement with nonfungible tokens (NFTs), witnessed by remarkable growth and development of different NFT marketplaces: gaming, metaverses, collectibles, art, and music, to name just a few. This book covers the early part of that movement, around the April 2021 timeframe, just before the massive market explosion just a few months later. The interviews contained within this book, looking back, were the early harbingers of that growth market. NFTs have grown dramatically since their inception, and even since April 2021. This book offers a taste of the new environment that

SOLD OUT IN FIFTEEN SECONDS

spawned what we see even growing further today.

This tenth book in the Crypto Hipster series, entitled **Sold Out in Fifteen Seconds** focuses on four Crypto Hipster podcasts. Darren Cullen, aka SER, CEO and Founder of Graffiti Kings, shares how his first NFT collectible offering in partnership with Our Planet sold out in fifteen seconds, and is the title of this book's inspirational story. Jillian Godsil, journalist, broadcaster, writer and former European Parliament candidate, and the Crypto Hipster conduct an NFT 101 discussion, covering topics like Beeple, Crypto Punks, music, and many more in an informative and educational discussion. Michael Dowling, finance professor at Dublin City University, shares his early research and insights into the metaverse and how we can create our own Digital Disneyland. And J.D. Salbego, Chief Executive Officer at AnRKey X talks about the early days of crypto gaming yield farming and his invention of Money Sports, a brand-new industry that has spawned in the eSports world because of blockchain technology.

My hope is that you find this book both educational and useful in your crypto and life journey.

Disclaimer: Most casual conversations in my podcasts were in the passive voice. To author this book and make it enjoyable, I have translated the content to the active voice as much as possible while maintaining the intent of my guests' answers and responses. I have provided links to all the original conversations at the beginning of each chapter. I welcome you to listen to the podcasts besides reading this book.

Chapter 1— How Graffiti Kings and Street Art are Capturing the NFT Art World's Attention and Trust

Graffiti Artist **Darren Cullen** aka **SER** from South London began his graffiti career way back in 1983 aged 10 years old, at the very birth of British graffiti. His path in graffiti started like many graffiti artists with the birth of hip-hop culture in the early 1980s. Exploring every aspect of the graffiti-writing scene SER found himself emblazoning his name across the streets and walls of London. This led to a greater need to increase his presence with the public and so began the systematic destruction of the train networks and rail infrastructure across the UK & the world. There then comes a point in every graffiti artist's life when their illegal activity becomes of great interest to the Police and having a prison cell as a second home is not that appealing so SER needed to rethink. This spurred SER into forming the Graffiti Kings collective with some of

SOLD OUT IN FIFTEEN SECONDS

the world's best graffiti & street artists to go legit and take on the world. Darren Cullen aka SER - Graffiti Kings founder/head honcho/artist

The only Graffiti Artist approved by the British Government & official Graffiti Artist for the London 2012 Games.... Just saying

Tel: 07877502506 / www.graffitikings.co.uk

Original Interview Date: May 8, 2021
Original Interview Link: https://spotifyanchor-web.app.link/e/o7UqFwYuavb

CRYPTO HIPSTER: Welcome to the Crypto Hipster Podcast. I have an amazing podcast for you today. I have an incredibly special guest. His name is Darren Cullen, aka SER. He is the founder and artist of Graffiti Kings. Darren, welcome to the show.

SER: Hello, sir. Good to be here.

SOLD OUT IN FIFTEEN SECONDS

CRYPTO HIPSTER: Great to have you. My first question to kick things off is, what is your background? And how does it relate to what you are doing now?

SER: I am a professional graffiti artist. Professional because I am now in endorsed by the British government for doing what I am doing. That came about in 1996. We were running diversionary projects with young children, keeping them off the streets and out of trouble. The British government, a department of the government called a D.E.T.R. came in and evaluated the projects that we were doing. They loved the projects that we were doing. And they authored a paper about it that was published in a report that went out to all local governments and endorsed what we did. It said if you have a problem with graffiti, this is a project that has been run successfully, and you should try to copy it or even still contact me. This is what many companies and the local governments did. Within days, weeks, afterwards, my phone just did

SOLD OUT IN FIFTEEN SECONDS

not stop. And that is when I went legit. I set up a limited company, Graffiti Kings, to take on this massive new workload that we were doing. Whereas before, it was just me. But now it just literally went mainstream. And since then, we've been working all over the world for funnily enough, every major brand there is, from painting their offices outside of their buildings, to tackling their advertising, billboards, and painting on the side of eight-story buildings, taking movie posters, and turning them into street art murals on the side of buildings, even down to painting kids' bedrooms. We do everything. If it can be painted, we are painting.

CRYPTO HIPSTER: What is graffiti art and street art?

SER: The media calls it Graffiti but we call it Writing. In Philadelphia, and in the Bronx, New York in the early 1970s, teenagers would write their names on the wall. They wrote a nickname on the wall. After their nickname, they would write a few

SOLD OUT IN FIFTEEN SECONDS

numbers. And those numbers would represent the bearers of where they lived in their town. And this phenomenon was one of writing. Then it came over to the U.K. in the early 1980s. And that is when I got into it in 1983 at 10 years of age. Obviously, the media got on top of it. Because in the 1970s in New York, you had graffiti. There has always been graffiti writing on the wall. As the media saw a new influx of writing on the wall, they just adopted the word graffiti.

We are called writers and the difference between graffiti, stroke writing, and street art is because we got into it as the second generation. The first generation were artists in Philadelphia and New York. They were doing it because of their nicknames and where they lived. They were marking their territory. And then we picked it up because of what they were doing. And what they were doing was vandalizing things. Anything that moved, or did not move, they would write their names on it. Whereas now, people are getting inspired and into this

SOLD OUT IN FIFTEEN SECONDS

culture, it is not through the vandalism side of it, it is through seeing the street art and nice colorful murals on the wall. So that is the difference. If you get into this space to vandalize, you are a graffiti artist or stroke writer. But if you get into this space because you want to create outstanding pieces of artworks that are colorful, then that is when you can call yourself a street artist.

CRYPTO HIPSTER: I remember I was big into the Philadelphia nightclub scene back in the early 1990s, so I know what you are talking about. I remember seeing those numbers on the wall and going to South Street and having a Philly cheesesteak.

What was your inspiration to get involved over in the U.K.?

SER: When I was in school, across the road from the school, there were these two brothers. And they had come back from a trip with their parents from

SOLD OUT IN FIFTEEN SECONDS

New York. And while they were out in New York, they had seen all the trains in the metro system, just literally blitz of all these pictures, cartoon characters, Donald Duck, Daffy Duck, all that sort of thing. They took photographs. Their mum and dad had explained to him what it was, and why they were doing it. They came back pretty clued up about what they had seen. And what it was about. They came to school and showed us these photographs of what they had taken, with all these glorious images on the trains and on the walls. And that was it. The bug had caught us.

Well, the reason it caught me as well is that I am not sure there could have been months, could have been weeks. But it was a period between when I had seen these photographs and when I saw the graffiti on the walls in my area. I remember one day for the first time, for example, walking behind the local saloon bars and on the walls around the back, where no one could see what was going on, just seeing these huge colorful paintings on the wall. I

SOLD OUT IN FIFTEEN SECONDS

was just amazed by it, just looking at it. Never seen in the free market before. Usually, if you see paintings on the wall, usually it is paintings of trees, nice scenery, or the countryside. Whereas this was very colorful, very dynamic, very abstract. I just remember seeing these paintings. And with the two brothers who had shown me these photographs. I put two and two together. I was like, "Wow, that's it!" That explained why these kids were doing it. That explained the kids had nicknames. Within seconds, we all adopted a nickname for ourselves. I called myself Flash. I think I have taken that from a comic book. I cannot remember why I called myself Flash. But that was my first tag.

From then on, we would go into the school, open the drawers, take all the marking pens, all the chalk, anything we could use to write our names on the walls. And that is what we did. And then it was not until maybe a few years later, around about 1984 or 1985, that you had a book that came out called *Subway Art*. And then you had the explosion of

SOLD OUT IN FIFTEEN SECONDS

MTV, and the video *Buffalo Girls* by Malcolm McLaren, and the film's style was about graffiti. That opened this whole new world. Before that, there was not much inspiration. For weeks, we would just copy these photographs and try to master drawing them. At first, it was not great. But it is like anything when you first play, like golf. In the beginning, it was not good. But you keep playing it, you keep painting; you get better. We just copied these photographs for months. We would get better drawings compared to what we were looking at. There was more inspiration after the Balkan films came out. It gave us an in-depth story about what it was, who it was, and where it was happening. And that just sparked the U.K. scene even more.

And I had gone to secondary school, and older, I was then at an age where I could jump on buses and leave my area. When I got into this, I was ten. But now, I am still young, I am still not traveling out of my area so much. We are still very local. Going to secondary school now and we are in an era where there are more people that know about this culture and have a meetup with other kids in the school. We are now jumping on buses and trains. And that is what we did every weekend, every night after school, just going around traveling and writing their name everywhere. That was it. And it just went on and went on and went on until I got the chance to manage these workshops and run these workshops for young adults to keep them off the streets. These diversionary projects, and that is all spawned into a professional thing.

CRYPTO HIPSTER: You recently had an art drop on the Wax platform that sold out in fifteen seconds. How did that entire process go? What is your secret to selling out so quickly?

SER: Well, luckily, we have a vast audience. The name is prominent, Graffiti Kings. But yes, so we have a great audience online. We have a Facebook audience of 2.4 million. We have viral videos that

SOLD OUT IN FIFTEEN SECONDS

have close to eighty million views and an average of forty million views. Do not get me wrong, I do not think most of my audience is purchasing these cards. This industry we are in is all Chinese for most people. Trying to get someone to talk to anyone about crypto is hard enough. Trying to talk to them about purchasing a JPEG is just another step out there in outer space.

We have been working extremely hard, very manic over the last few months, non-stop. No sleep, hardly any sleep, just contacting. Again, it is what we do in the real world. Trying to draw up business, trying to draw up collaborations, it is just literally just contacting companies sending out decks, explaining what we can do for them. And, yes, that is exactly what we have done in this space. We have reached out to various brands in the cryptoverse, explained who we are, explained what we want to do. This arena speaks out to us, crying out for us. It is digital. I have been here in this digital world since the birth of Yahoo Messenger. We reached out to

SOLD OUT IN FIFTEEN SECONDS

Our Planet, explained who we were and what we are doing. They loved what we were doing. And they said, Yes, let us give it a go. And the first drop was six thousand, which is small. But now that I know because a neck and neck strap that we have in on the 22nd of May, with we have around 30,000 packs. So hopefully, more people will get the chance. After these sold out in 15 seconds, our Twitter page just literally blew up with unhappy people that could not purchase any of these cards. Hopefully, this time now more people will get it. We reached out and said, Look, this is what we want to do. They liked it. And within a few weeks, we did not sleep, just got our heads down, and designed all these great new cards. And then it went like that. We just sold out in fifteen seconds.

CRYPTO HIPSTER: So, you had one drop already. You are going to have a second drop coming up soon?

SOLD OUT IN FIFTEEN SECONDS

SER: The second drop is we have our two collectibles. That is a collaboration we have been working on for quite a few months. Whereas *Our Planet* collaboration is very new. I reached out to them just recently and said that we are doing this drop. We have our two collectibles coming up and we have been doing other things in the NFT space for other people. It would be a great collaboration. We could do stuff together. That happened innocently. It happened all in a tiny window. And the one we got producing collectibles, that is another fabulous drop. It is different, and it is called the Crypto Moon Boys.

That was what we started again. With *Our Planet* collaboration, you have graffiti art where the Graffiti Kings created outstanding pieces of artwork. And then, our second collection is just us as artists, creating NFTs that are going to be in a pack as a celebration of the artwork that we created at Graffiti Kings. That second collection is a new world that we have created called the Crypto Moon

SOLD OUT IN FIFTEEN SECONDS

Boys. Within these Crypto Moon Boys, we have three gangs. One gang, called the Huddle Warriors, features a character called the Bitcoin Kid and Bit Boy and various other characters. The next gangs are called the Crypto Bulls and the Crypto Bears. These three gangs are fighting each other, trying to be the winners of the new metaverse before the great reset in 2030 comes along. And one of them wants to reign supreme. So that is the story we have with the Crypto Moon Boys. We have grand designs. Have a look. That is the Arpanet drop we have coming up. We feature the artwork ourselves and what created no one has seen yet. This artwork we painted on the wall. And as soon as we painted them, we painted over them. Therefore, no one has seen them. They are going to be exclusive just for the drop.

CRYPTO HIPSTER: You have made it a point that customer service is King. Over the last decade, there were a lot of industries here in the U.S. that

SOLD OUT IN FIFTEEN SECONDS

replaced customer service with nothing. Customer service was commoditized and is now missing.

What have you been able to achieve and learn that would not have been possible if you had not focused on customer service first?

SER: I do not get it. I take it the same as breathing air. This is normal. Treating people one on one with respect. And that is another reason we are where we are. Whereas other people in this space, doing what I am doing, are just conducting the artwork. Most people in this space, in my world, are just agencies. They have no background in what it is they are selling. They are just someone trying to make a profit. And they are taking an email from a client from their nicely created website, which they stick online and make it look like what it is supposed to look like. And they get a job, come in, and they just go through their list of artists, pick one and say, look, here is a job, do it. Whereas from the first email, we work out what the client wants and we will have a conversation. A person will always collaborate directly with the artist, right from the start, right through to the end of executing the project. Because this is what we do as a hobby. I mean, we were privileged to know that we are getting paid as artists. We are lucky to be paid as an artist full stop, especially at our age. And I am in my mid-forties.

CRYPTO HIPSTER: I understand that because my focus is on customer service and building relationships and that is the way to build business. You also said vandalism saved you from a life of crime. How would you inspire or direct artists to use their gifts and help them channel their gifts positively towards a life based on their creative skills?

SER: Whether it is graffiti or creating memes, which is a hot topic now, for years and years, we have been looking at these memes and laughing and thinking they are fun. We pass them on, and we

SOLD OUT IN FIFTEEN SECONDS

share them, thinking they have no value. Whereas now these memes are generating so much attention and value. When you think about them, they make you smile; they make you laugh, that is a winner. Straight away. It is emotional. If you want to get into this space, I encourage people straight away to join groups, Facebook being a significant starting point. That is if you are a graffiti artist, or you are an abstract artist, or, or even your pottery artist, you create, you know, you want to create pottery, take photographs, and create photographs of your pottery. I guarantee you there is going to be industry in this space for every arena. You can even think of penguins, if you like penguins, or taking photographs of penguins... someone is going to buy a photograph of a penguin.

Find these groups on Facebook. Just be engaged in talking about your ideas, explaining your ideas, and you are going to get a load of hate. You cannot please everyone. There is not one person in this world who can please everyone. Get yourself into

SOLD OUT IN FIFTEEN SECONDS

these groups. Explain what you are doing. Hopefully, find other people that will help you fight, give you advice, and offer some help. And then you might even find people that like what you are doing and may want to join. And if that is the case, I will encourage that. Collaboration is key. You have so many struggling artists in the world. They are all just trying to do it on their own. There is too much work involved for anyone to do with two hands. Get yourself into a team. I encourage people to try that. At least try it. If you do not you will not know until you try. And yes, if you get knocked back quickly, do not take that as the last thing that is going to happen. Try. Try again. Give it at least three or four or four chances before you knock the idea on the head of working with someone. It may just be that the first person you worked with was not right for you. Hopefully, your gut instinct will kick in. I say that because they are young, and they do not understand how that feels. But just keep trying.

SOLD OUT IN FIFTEEN SECONDS

On Facebook, reach out to as many people and explain what you are doing. Create some magnificent pieces of artwork and get yourself online and see what happens. And once you get online, do not just think it is that easy. Do not just post it and forget about it. You must do what big brands do: marketing. And in my case, do not sleep, create the artwork, stick online. And do not sleep until you get as many people to see it and talk about it. Because if people have not seen it and are talking about it, then no one can hear you and you are still no one. You must get people talking and engaged in social media. That is why everyone here enjoys sharing. You need to get all that going. And again, do not be afraid to get the negative responses, which you are going to get course. Like I said, you cannot please everyone. The best artwork in the world still gets negative reviews. Expect a lot of hate. In my case, that hate is good. There is no such thing as bad news. Just do not stop doing it. Just do not stop.

SOLD OUT IN FIFTEEN SECONDS

CRYPTO HIPSTER: I agree. How could NFT's be the basis for a new society where people have equity and are building the future? How would you See how would you envision a world like that looking?

SER: Well, just by looking at what I am seeing already, *Our Planet* collaboration, where if you are if you are lucky enough to own these rare NFTs, you can stake them on games and get rewards for staking them. And you are getting paid. Sometimes, as an example, artist Ken Bozak, if you are lucky enough to own one NFT by him, and you can stake it on *Our Planet*, you can generate 20,000 pounds a year. 20,000 pounds may not change your life, but you can sit down comfortably, not having to worry about going to work if you do not want.

And there is a difference between having a career, doing what you want to do, or if you do not have a career, then that means you have a job. That is a different thing. If you want a career, you need to dedicate your time to doing what you want to do. If

SOLD OUT IN FIFTEEN SECONDS

you do not have that, then you are working, and that is a job. As I am concerned, if you got into it, you could be able to sit on your bum and put 24 hours into this space and make it work for you, rather than trying to work for someone else. That is what NFTs are doing for 1000s of people already that are staking these NFTs on a game and getting rewards from it. Ridiculous. I sold my house to get into this space. I saw where this was going. I was like, Okay; we need to get into this space as this new in fourth industrial revolution, because it is going to swallow up the world.

CRYPTO HIPSTER: Thank you very much for your time. I congratulate you on your recent drop. I am looking forward to the next one to see how fast that goes. And my last question is, if anybody wants to contact you, to find out more information about you, to have you prepare some artwork for them, how can they contact you?

SOLD OUT IN FIFTEEN SECONDS

SER: Just go online search for Graffiti Kings. We will be the first ones to pop up. And we will be the second and the third and the fourth and fifth and so on. Just go on to the contact page and send us a nice, happy email with a smile at the end. And yes, that gets my attention.

Chapter 2— NFTs for Dummies

For the 2021 International Women's Day, **Jillian Godsil** was nominated one of one hundred global women in leadership awards.

Last June, she was awarded the 2020 Blockchain Journalist by *Uptrends* (largest blockchain social platform). In 2019 Jillian was nominated for the national IMRO radio awards for her *East Coast FM* Saturday morning show and was awarded the 2019 AI and Blockchain Journalist of the Year at the CC Forum in London. She is an enthusiastic advocate for blockchain, a seasoned professional in fintech and internationally recognized champion for equality – whether in homelessness, gender, or the law.

Jillian has held senior positions with global PR companies in Sydney, Singapore, London, and Dublin. She was PRO of Iona Technologies (Ireland's first company to float on NASDAQ). She changed the law in Ireland in 2014 and is a former European Parliamentary candidate (as an independent).

She is a co-founder and journalist in Blockleaders.io. She freelances for Irish Tech News, Irish Central, The Irish Independent and The Irish Times. She has her own radio shows on *Dublin City FM* and *East Coast FM* – she was nominated for a national radio award, the IMRO, in 2019. Her first job after graduating from Trinity College was as a systems analyst with JP Morgan.

She is advisor to several ICOs, has been named a Crypto Queen by In Zero Conferences as well as listed in the fifty most influential women in the global blockchain rollcall. She is named amongst the top ten people in Blockchain in Ireland. She was voted into the top twenty global Hedera Hashgraph Ambassadors in 2018. She is a board member of EOS Dublin. She is a community leader for

SOLD OUT IN FIFTEEN SECONDS

Algorand. She is chain agnostic while she loves blockchain.

She has been shortlisted for the Image Businesswoman of Year and shortlisted for Woman of the Year by Women in IT in 2018. She made the top one hundred Global Blockchain Leaders list for 2019 for the Lattice80 report.

Jillian is enthusiastic about getting women into blockchain – democratizing opportunity for all women. She was awarded the Order of Merit by the President of Liberland.

Pre COVID - She keynotes and chairs blockchain events around the world – including Kyiv, Austin, Muscat, Columbo, Dubai, Cape Town, Liberland, Malta, Amsterdam, Vienna, Dublin, and London. Now this work is virtual from her sleepy backwater village in rural Ireland.

Original Interview Date: March 26, 2021

SOLD OUT IN FIFTEEN SECONDS

Original Interview Link: https://spotifyanchor-web.app.link/e/OyHMVp1vavb

CRYPTO HIPSTER: Hello, everybody. I have an amazing podcast for you today. Ms. Jillian Godsil. She is the founder and chief executive officer of Block Leaders, and she has authored a book entitled, *Persons of Interest*. Jillian, welcome to the show.

Jillian: Thank you for having me.

CRYPTO HIPSTER: What is your background? And how does it relate directly to today's conversation regarding a boiling topic, nonfungible tokens (NFTs)?

Jillian: Well, I am a hot person. I am very fluid. My background is I have 30 years of FinTech experience. My first job was with JP Morgan in London. I worked there for three years. I have even worked in Australia. And then in Singapore in

SOLD OUT IN FIFTEEN SECONDS

FinTech, although it was called advanced technology back in those days, because it was the Dark Ages. And then I came back to Ireland and worked for a software company. An incredibly famous Irishman once floated on that stick. My life stopped, which was also granted. And I was wondering what this new FinTech stuff is, right? Then I hit divorce and recession, and neither was planned. Never go through divorce during the recession, it is bad timing. The banks took away my home. And there were bailiffs and a lot of crazy stuff. And I became very activated, and I changed the law because I was a ranting anti banker. I proclaimed the world must be a better place than this. So, I changed the law because there are many old-fashioned laws. I was challenging old-fashioned attitudes towards financial failure.

And then I ran the 2014 European Parliamentary elections as an Independent, and I got 11,000 votes, of which I am so proud. Not enough to get elected, but enough to make a difference. And then my life

SOLD OUT IN FIFTEEN SECONDS

ended. Then all was quiet. Okay, that is me. I am done. I have done my moment in the sun. I have had my career. I have my children, you know, that is it. And then about a year later, I met blockchain. Oh, now I know how I can change the world and make the world a better place! Do all those things, ambitions that I had throughout my career that did never really took off. And I remember I hit the.com stuff. I was right in the middle of that, and I loved it. And it was clever because innovation was really rethinking stuff. But it is not about the money. The thing that blockchain does is that it democratizes opportunity and access.

When I met blockchain, it made sense. I chucked myself into the deep end. I went off to Kyiv to chair a blockchain fashion at the blockchain conference. On the way over, I read a lot. And it has been crazy ever since. It has been amazing ever since. And then, as we know, NFTs are the next progression. There are so many progressions of blockchain, including decentralized finance, but NFTs have been around for a while. They are just now coming into the room and they are powerful in upsetting the apple carts.

CRYPTO HIPSTER: What are nonfungible tokens (NFTs)?

Jillian: In some ways, it is almost easier to ask what fungible tokens are rather than nonfungible tokens. Most of the world is nonfungible. You and I are nonfungible. You cannot divide us in half and we are not equally swappable. Something like a fungible token is money, for example. Money is an excellent example of a fungible token because if I have $1, and you have $1, we can swap them, or I can even break down the dollar into coins. We can still swap the same value, but nonfungible tokens are things that cannot be swapped like for like. It is a unique entity.

The problem before blockchain is that it was extremely hard to have unique or solitary items in digital asset formats because things can be copied and shared and emailed all over the place. I may email you a picture of something. Blockchain has allowed that uniqueness so we can share the things from real life and those things can maintain their uniqueness. If there is a tree in your garden, there is not another tree like it, we can now identify that tree in the digital world. You can say there are only one or several ones if you want to have multiple authenticated copies. NFTs are quite clever, really. It is bringing the real world into the digital world.

CRYPTO HIPSTER: How do these nonfungible tokens work?

Jillian: Blockchain as a technology is powerful, and it is immutable. It is possible to mint something on the blockchain. I will mention this coaster here because it is a unique coaster and I own it. And I can mint it onto the blockchain since I am the owner. And if I wanted to sell it or exchange it, the blockchain preserves the provenance. We can follow the coaster around the world using blockchain technology if it is sold multiple times and travels the globe.

CRYPTO HIPSTER: Where can I buy them? In the USA, we have some exchanges. We have Gemini. We have Coinbase. None of them is where you can buy an NFT token fungible token. Is there a special exchange to buy it?

Jillian: NFTs are not cryptocurrencies, they are assets. They are crypto assets because they are created through cryptography, making them unique, but they are not coins. You will not see them exchanged as tokens on an exchange, or not. But they are an asset. So, if you want to buy them, there are many platforms that have sprung up. There's Open Sea and Wax platform. There are many of them where people create their NFTs and sell them or share them sometimes. If you have an NFT, you can get an AirDrop. The whole AirDrop notion within the crypto world is you can get cards

SOLD OUT IN FIFTEEN SECONDS

and NFTs sent to you. And in fact, I sold my first NFT a little while ago, two weeks ago, and it was a tweet. Do you remember how Jack Dorsey sold his tweet for $6 million? Yes, the founder of Twitter sold his tweet. It was the first tweet he wrote. I sold my tweet. And it was a recent tweet that I had written and I got $10 for it. I sold it to a friend who bought it, so that is called insider trading, but it was fun. My first NFT could be valuable in the future. Who knows?

CRYPTO HIPSTER: How else can we use NFTs in our daily lives? This seems like you can do a lot of things with them.

Jillian: I want to talk about music. The NFT is interesting at this stage for artists, although your daily life we will come back to in a minute. If you are a musical artist typically, how do you make your money back? The oldest compilations, CDs, tapes, vinyl, and LPs musicians made their money through touring and merchandizing. Then streaming. Of

SOLD OUT IN FIFTEEN SECONDS

course, streaming is not great for artists because they make a fraction of the amount. They really must have an enormously famous name to make any money from streaming. You could have millions of people downloading your music and nobody gives you a penny. This is ridiculous. And why streaming works is because it is convenient. If you and I want to buy music, of course we are going to buy streaming music because it is not expensive, it is convenient, and we do not pay much attention to so little of it goes back to the musician. We do it because most people are law-abiding, at least the streaming is legal. But what companies like Spotify have done is that they have eviscerated musicians. They do not make any money from it and they do not see the value of the download to the money that they earn.

Think of NFTs instead. The Kings of Leon recently proved this when they announced their eighth album, and if you are a fan, it is not groundbreaking, except they did an NFT. They did a

SOLD OUT IN FIFTEEN SECONDS

quirky thing where when you buy their new album, they will also ship you off a vinyl and attach an NFT. They did a finite number of NFTs at auction time. I am not sure which way it worked. But I know that Kings of Leon will take most of that money and give most of it to charity, to groupies, and to roadies. Roadies do not make any money in the non-gig economy. NFTs for the roadies mean money. But most of the income from that sale goes to the artist. With NFTs, the money goes to the artist where it should go, because they created it.

And then ordinary people, where it gets exciting, is an NFT can be anything. An NFT can be an access point. You can sell an NFT. If you want to get into a nightclub in London, you can buy or sell an NFT ticket. And the wonderful thing about the NFT tickets is you can do a digital ticket and authenticate it so it is not duplicated or counterfeited. The beauty of that is that the person uses that ticket to gain access to the club. But also, there's other things because it is an NFT in your

SOLD OUT IN FIFTEEN SECONDS

wallet. They can send you live action or drama. Say, there is a roving photographer that night, and they take photographs. You have a photo shot done at a famous entrance. They can send you that picture as an NFT that is your proof you were there. If you have an NFT, the club or the artist who is there can send you stuff afterwards. Say I am an up-and-coming DJ in the club, and you come with your NFT, I can also just send you photographs of me from the night with you and me both there. I send children NFT stuff, and so you are creating a bond.

NFTs can be just a unique thing. It is a unique digital item and there are so many uses coming forward. Are you following metaverses? Metaverses are parallel universes in the digital world. Somebody recently said, "Oh, Elon Musk. He wants to go to Mars." That is cool. Because it costs a lot of money, most of us will never get to Mars. Most of our children will not get to Mars. But what if you could go to Mars in the metaverse and really enjoy it? That possibility is becoming much more lifelike and interesting. I am not saying do not go out into nature, breathe the loving air, and look at the flowers and the trees. But go off for a bit of fun in your life on Mars in the metaverse. With the Upland project, they are mapping their world to the real world. All the household properties in that metaverse are NFTs. I was speaking to one founder, and he said to look around. What exemplifies an NFT more than a house, as every property is unique? We know that even if you build one property in a tower block of hundreds of properties, your unit is unique. So? NFTs can be anything digital.

CRYPTO HIPSTER: I guess you can use NFTs for anything?

Jillian: Yes. It is only really limited by our imaginations... by our imaginations and by the demand. It is not enough to have an idea. You want someone else to buy into it. And then you are off. It is exciting because anyone can listen to this and

SOLD OUT IN FIFTEEN SECONDS

have an idea. When I was interviewing the Upland founder, Dan, I said I would not mind having a bookshop or an art gallery in the metaverse. I will not have a physical store or gallery, but I could have one in a metaverse. We could have fun and hang out there. You know, I love Mondays and Tuesdays. And I can Oh, I can be as beautiful as I want to be as well. Another wonderful thing. I can choose my avatar of who I could be. I do not know who my idol is, but I could be that swan around my bookshop. It would be fun.

CRYPTO HIPSTER: Talking about fun, there is a mania going on in the market right now. You know, some comparisons have been made in the past between Bitcoin and Tulip Mania. Now, others have called NFTs pure money laundering. Realistically, what do you think is causing the NFT market to explode now? And how legitimate are these NFTs? Because there have been accusations about money laundering?

SOLD OUT IN FIFTEEN SECONDS

Jillian: Yes, there was recently a famous sale at Christie's and there have been lots of articles written about it. The source of funds for the purchase was for a different purpose. There are a lot of moving parts. We do not know what is happening. It is such big money. I mean, it is crazy.

People spend a lot of money on van Gough's and other art, art classes, and collectibles. So, is it a bubble? I do not think so. What is interesting for me is that, for artists, first off, it is amazing. There is a lot of fun. You can do something flashy and sell it. And then for people who want to get into this, I was listening to an interview by Andreas Antonopoulos, who is an original Bitcoin man, talking about whether it is too late to buy Bitcoin. Because one Bitcoin is $60,000 on any day. For most people, buying a whole Bitcoin is too expensive. And they were talking about buying, well do not buy one, just buy your fifty euros worth, whatever it is, and just put it away in your children's education. But for people who do not

SOLD OUT IN FIFTEEN SECONDS

want to buy a bit of Bitcoin, why not buy an NFT? And then, why would you buy an NFT instead of a piece of art, or, if you are a gamer, all those skins and tools? Those things strengthen you, and make you faster, cleverer, or better in your game. But if it is just a piece of our afternoon, why would you bother doing that? If you turn that around and see how much of our day is spent online, then why not buy an NFT?

I love the outside. I am just back from the beautiful countryside. It is sunny here. It is spring. The daffodils are up. It is beautiful. We spend so much more time online; we should have beautiful things online. That is why people are buying NFT's because they can.

CRYPTO HIPSTER: talked about people spending a lot of money. There is an artist and art fan in Singapore. His name is Vignesh Sundaresan. (MetaKoven). He is living in Little India in Singapore. He paid $69 million for an art piece

SOLD OUT IN FIFTEEN SECONDS

entitled *Everydays: The First 5000 Days* created by Beeple. Are we just conducting crowdfunding? Is this just another way of crowdfunding in the art world for crypto assets? How do you see that?

Jillian: A lot has been written about that sale, and I understand rightly or wrongly, but there is a method behind the madness and that purchase. Justin Sun from TRON went to buy it and his bid did not get through, which he thought should have gone through. There could be a method for that. As you buy something, throw a spotlight on something else, which would make the investment in that sixty-nine million not such a crazy purchase. Because you are going to use it for another purpose if you like, so that is an extreme case, but a lot of ordinary artists are earning good money.

Some people are earning a couple of Ethereum for their artwork, which is not bad. I would not mind doing that. That would be genuinely nice. If you are an artist too, and no one's going to galleries, or

SOLD OUT IN FIFTEEN SECONDS

hanging your pictures up in restaurants or buildings, earning a couple of Ethereum sounds like a good deal. We spend a lot of money on expensive things. If you want to buy a niece piece of art, look at Crypto Punks. I am so jealous. They were all given away for free at the start. I wish I had been there. I came too late. I am so jealous. I have just an ordinary avatar on my Twitter. I have Crypto Punk envy. I cannot spend all my money on one.

CRYPTO HIPSTER: What are Crypto Punks?

Jillian: It was a program and there were about ten thousand of them. They used an algorithm to produce slightly different variants. Crypto Punks are like little Lego style heads and shoulders. And then who received the drop on Ethereum got them for free, but then a lot of them have been selling since. And some punks are selling for quite a lot of money. If you had been there early, you would have gotten them for free, which I missed. They are very

SOLD OUT IN FIFTEEN SECONDS

distinctive. If you go onto your social media, you see all these heads. And that's Crypto Punks.

CRYPTO HIPSTER: Well, you know, speaking of jealousy, you said a word bubble earlier. Are we working under a bubble? And if not, you know, what would drive the crypto market forward?

Jillian: Anything that raises the conversation about crypto blockchain to the rest of the world is a good thing. Even when it is a terrible thing, it is a good thing. We have moved away from the dark web and Ponzi schemes to looking at things, so even a bubble is not inherently fraudulent. In a bubble, something is perceived to have a greater value, and that value may not last. If you purchase it, it may not be valuable in the future. And that is from everything from art houses to designer handbags. It is different when people are going to sell you something. It is worth whatever someone wants to pay for it.

SOLD OUT IN FIFTEEN SECONDS

I read an article recently by a friend of mine, an online friend. And she was giving off yards about International Women's Day and said, "Oh, it's like a big Valentine's Day and everyone's Wonder Woman." And she is wrong. The day is International Women's Rights Day. As opposed to saying we have glorious women in our lives, our mothers, our sisters, or our bosses, it is about the rights that are attached to it, and that women are not paid the same as men. Unless we have the need for rights, there will not be a conversation. And equality is part of the blockchain conversation. Anything that brings this conversation into the mainstream is good, even if we can look back and say that was weird. So, it is exciting now. But if you do not have conversations like women's rights, and mental health for example, and even weird stuff like NFTs, it raises the topic. Anything that raises the topic and brings it mainstream, I am all for it.

CRYPTO HIPSTER: Me too. Right now, there has been talk by some people that have asked about

SOLD OUT IN FIFTEEN SECONDS

investing in the stock market in the U.S. being not based on fundamentals anymore, based on hype, while some people only have access to lottery tickets. And if they can have access to a crypto asset instead and invest in something that has long-term potential, then wouldn't that be best for them and for the economy?

Jillian: That is an excellent point. A huge point is if you are rich, money flows to the rich, and it has increasingly done so this century. It is terrible how income equalities have grown and grown and grown. And crypto assets offer an opportunity for people to invest if they wish to advance faster. It opens the door to people having a look at other things. You might buy that little Crypto Punk or something else for small money that could become worth a lot of money. That ability for people to invest in things that might become more valuable has been nonexistent. Unless you are super rich, you cannot buy an apartment. And especially in places like downtown Manhattan, you just do not have an opportunity. I am not suggesting that there is no financial advice, but NFTs could be a fun thing to take a punt on money you can afford to lose on something that is fun and accessible. Ten years down the track or ten months down the track, you could sell it and make a profit from it.

CRYPTO HIPSTER: Could you tell me a little about your most recent book?

Jillian: I write a lot of interviews. I love feature writing. I love this industry, because I get to talk to all the important people who are creating businesses and working in this space. And it is really fascinating. It is an access you would not ordinarily get because it is a nascent industry. I recently wanted to interview somebody who is remarkably high profile in the traditional world. And author a book about values. And I approached through the book, the book promotion. It is a regular approach. But they went no, no, totally no. Whereas if I went to somebody who is huge in this

SOLD OUT IN FIFTEEN SECONDS

crypto space, I get access to them. And I can interview them, which is a great privilege for me. There are about forty people in here that I have interviewed, and it is all about who they are. I like to understand who people are behind the projects, because that makes them more interested in a product or project. But who they are and why they do it is interesting. I launched this last year. personsofinterest.io is the website. But I am making it into an NFT on the Near protocol website. I have forty-two illustrations, and I am going to make them into NFTs and launch them on Wax at the end of next month.

CRYPTO HIPSTER: How can people find more information about you contact you? How can they do that?

Jillian: LinkedIn is the best thing for me. LinkedIn says my name, Julian also with a G and A G. And it is the easiest thing to find me and I publish a lot of my stuff. I am on Twitter too, as well. But LinkedIn

SOLD OUT IN FIFTEEN SECONDS

is and I write for voice and blog theaters, and I write for it. And I obviously do podcasts here too, as well. But LinkedIn is the best place to catch me, I think.

SOLD OUT IN FIFTEEN SECONDS

Chapter 3— Stepping into the Metaverse: Building Digital Disneyland

Michael Dowling is a Professor of Finance at Dublin City University Business School. Before returning to Ireland in 2020, Michael established and managed the AI Business research center in Rennes School of Business, France. The first artificial intelligence for business research center in Europe. Building on that his research explores the intersection between financial behavior and technology.

He has published the first studies on non-fungible token (NFT) markets, including research on the rise of NFT metaverses. These metaverses, or virtual worlds based on the blockchain, evoke memories of classic sci-fi virtual worlds such as Neal Stephenson's *Snow Crash*.

SOLD OUT IN FIFTEEN SECONDS

Michael tweets at @MichaelMDowling on twitter. His profile is available at: https://www.dcu.ie/researchsupport/research-profile?PERSON_ID=1590232 or LinkedIn: search - Michael Dowling DCU.

Original Interview Date: April 30, 2021
Original Interview Link: https://spotifyanchor-web.app.link/e/GlkbJ4hxavb

CRYPTO HIPSTER: Welcome today to my guest, a professor at the Dublin City University School of Business. Welcome to the show, Michael Dowling.

Michael: Thank you. Great to be here.

CRYPTO HIPSTER: My first question for you is, what is your background? And how does it relate to what you are doing now?

Michael: I did my PhD in Behavioral Finance. I heard people make behavioral decisions in finance.

SOLD OUT IN FIFTEEN SECONDS

Not too many people were interested in that idea, because there was a U.S. philosophy that the market will correct any individual mistake or bias. But FinTech helped that area explode in terms of popularity, because with FinTech, you are trying to tailor your message to individual behaviors. That came to a head about five years ago. I left Ireland to go to France. And there I was working on a mixture of behavior, technology, and helping to set up and roll out a large research center on artificial intelligence. I spent the last few years doing this and crypto just kept popping up. Even though crypto is not artificial intelligence, you just cannot look at modern finance without crypto popping in.

I have published a few studies on crypto and it was all very normal stuff. But then, as we all know, the Covid lockdown happened about a year ago. My wife and I remember we were listening to a speech by the U.K. Prime Minister and he said many people are going to die. Hundreds of 1000s may die, he said, in a horrific speech. We left our small

SOLD OUT IN FIFTEEN SECONDS

apartment in quite rural France and we escaped out to the countryside; we got a cottage surrounded by a forest. And then lockdown was announced, and we spent the next months in the forest. The first few days we wandered around pointing at trees and then just incredible boredom kicked in.

I used that time to take a thorough analysis into crypto, and not just what I have done before in academic studies. I enjoyed reading about everything around it, like what is the philosophy around crypto, and started trading as a way of making money while in my little cottage in the French wilderness. Then we moved back to Dublin in September 2021 as I took at position and ditched all my material that I had built up. So, I sold everything I had built during the wilderness days and then just watched the market climb after I sold all my crypto at lower prices. Ethereum price is much higher now, over $2000 per coin, but I continually watch the price, like a sadistic way of working out how much I lost or could have had.

SOLD OUT IN FIFTEEN SECONDS

And then, with the new lockdown in Ireland, we do not have a house since we arrived here about five months ago.

And that's when NFTs took off and I jumped into those entities like chemistry, playing games using NFT characters where you buy characters your audience is familiar with. These unique items are registered on the blockchain and might be part of the game, might be artwork. And I experimented with them. Then it occurred to me because it is my actual job, I could just do some interesting research here. I published the first paper on NFT pricing, got a huge reception in like Bloomberg and have been adjusting and diving deeper into NFTs since then, expanding my knowledge. And we are here today talking to each other.

CRYPTO HIPSTER: Great. Yeah, I had Ethereum too, and I sold it off and I went a different route. One is decentralized finance (DeFi). And I bought a lot of DeFi tokens. The other one is NFTs, with which you

SOLD OUT IN FIFTEEN SECONDS

are involved. The question I have that is related to NFTs is what is a metaverse?

Michael: One of the first things that I did from the start with looking at NFTs and all the raw data was I looked at all the places where NFTs are being created. And it is quite clear, there are three distinct categories of NFTs. Art and collectibles that have taken all the news coverage, but there's NFTs related to gaming. You get your universe and you build up your characters, your axiom fantasies, and your little blobs that are fighting each other. And then you have your metaverse NFTs, photos, and virtual worlds. Many people who have read Neil Stevenson are motivated by a book called *Snow Crash*, about the slightly declining negative physical world. Many people have crappy jobs but then go home and they log into the metaverse and it is a virtual world where you can be honest, and there are no class barriers that stop you from doing good things. The metaverse does not have the physical gravity of real life, so the possibilities are endless.

SOLD OUT IN FIFTEEN SECONDS

That is where the term comes from the meta-variety. And that is the core idea. It is like this virtual world, where people can live in now that is now hybrid because with an NFT you own the land. Individual parts of the land can be owned with a restricted number of parcels. You can buy an NFT, build your plot of land wherever you want, and have a say in the world's running. And the opportunity and the promise of the metaverse is this idea of living in a world where we can do remarkable things, or at the very least be entertained.

CRYPTO HIPSTER: What could the metaverse real estate market become or what do you envision of that world being and how do we get there?

Michael: There are a few different schools of thought on this. Let us go back to the mindset of those people based on movies about people who set out exploring the Wild West and trying to find places to explore and live and mine for gold. If it was not a good place to live, then there was like an endless choice of places for them to go. And that is the best way of approaching the concept of a metaverse. There will be some sort of metaverse chain in the future where there is a Genesis Metaverse that you can fork and create a custom metaverse and then populate it with your own ideas. We do not have the concept of scarcity to deal with in the metaverse like we do with art, or with twenty-one million Bitcoin. We have stereotypes about how we have chosen to live our lives in this physical world. I do not know. We might want to break down a bit and start thinking about how we might want to live in a metaverse. It is not really that technically difficult to imagine.

A metaverse type chain that people can fork is a realistic possibility. We see this with normal games, where they buy an engine, like the Unreal Engine, and then they develop games on that core. But what we are going to see is an explosion of ideas for what people want these virtual worlds to be. Despite some of the negativity that permeates daily life, we are aiming towards the future for people will have a lot more time to spend on entertainment. If you look day to day, the world looks worrying. If you look year to year, it is okay, but if you look decade to decade, the world is objectively getting much better. And it is as we are moving into this thing where maybe automation is out to kill a lot more jobs and can free up a lot more time.

Then maybe we consider these new ways of being entertained by living in these virtual worlds. We are going to see developing choices we are seeing now, like the current worlds that exist in Decentraland, for example, where the currency called Mana was worth about 1.7 billion euro this morning. We do not have a world size, but it is worthy of thoughtful consideration. It is not just an idea that someone is thinking of in the car on their drive to work in the morning. I mean, metaverses are serious enterprises that are becoming a series of values.

CRYPTO HIPSTER: With your research, what have you learned not just from a technological perspective, but from a social perspective? What, socially, are some unique insights you could share that other people did not know about?

Michael: I have published a paper called *Fertile Land*, which looks at the pricing of land in Decentraland. I was questioning whether there was some sort of rhyme or reason to how land is priced one day or another in the metaverse. It is hard to see logic based just on how everything has gone early on. That was the first study. The second study I was looking at, given that it is crypto investors, was how people are using their spare money to invest in NFTs. Is there some relationship? Is there a relationship between the rising price of Bitcoin and the rise of Decentraland or Crypto Punks? And from my research, both are entirely different asset classes.

SOLD OUT IN FIFTEEN SECONDS

With standard finance locked down, it is just like normal behavior happening here. What it means is, there's loads of different ideas going on, and we do not need things to be rational from the very beginning. It is great having loads of debates and loads of discussions. One on extreme you have critics who claim because the metaverse is just a piece of code, it is worth nothing; anybody can create a code and it is worth noting. And, in contrast, believers claim this is the future of society and we will move towards this virtual world. These are massive debates that are happening. No wonder the pricing is all over the place. I am a little confined, despite my financial behavior research, by just the behavioral finance mindset, which is really getting rows of numbers and seeing if they have a relationship with each other. That is why I enjoy buying a bit of land.

I bought some land in The Sandbox. I do not know if that world is going to do anything. But once you buy the land, it has an interesting fence. It gives you

SOLD OUT IN FIFTEEN SECONDS

a plot of land, and you lock in your Metamask and you do what you want to make with your land. They provide you with la game design, to build a digital Disneyland. You are trying to design an adult version of ROBLOX, and it is all about designing a game. My wife and I were sitting down to eat when we tucked our kids in bed, and we were thinking about what we had learned. The metaverse changes your perspective. I was just listening to MetaKoven, the guy who bought the famous Beeple painting. His original name was King of the Metaverse and he was buying metaverse land. He was just speaking about the possibility of these metaverses from a non-investor philosophic sense. He says these are worlds where everybody can experience everything, many of the things that he did not experience as a kid. My insight from his speech is we need a lot more social involvement. And you log into the metaverse, and a lot of these worlds are greener pastures where you wander around. The first thing people talk about is their currency, but you do not

SOLD OUT IN FIFTEEN SECONDS

go to the Barbados tourism website to talk about the Dollar. You go to Barbados to enjoy the beaches.

And this is something that is quite interesting to see. This thinking just makes much more philosophical sense than investing sense. And that is the key insight. Do not over-analyze the numbers or do not have it make perfect sense right now. If you can imagine something happening here, then it will happen in the future in the metaverse.

CRYPTO HIPSTER: How do you feel that these virtual lands can become mainstream?

Michael: Don't begrudge anybody, whatever keeps them entertained is good. Real art is a terrible investment. The reason few people invest in normal art is that it is not a wonderful investment. And I am not sure why people fall into the trap of thinking that if something has been digitalized, and some attributes taken away from us, it now has more value. My wife is Russian. And in Russia, the idea is

SOLD OUT IN FIFTEEN SECONDS

you have your Dutch countryside house that you go to every weekend, and everybody has art from a Dutch painter. But if everybody has this countryside house, we think Metaverse is like that person's virtual house, where they have their friends together in a virtual village. And they have an activity that generates wealth in their virtual world that enables them to have virtual entertainment. And people can go to countryside retreats or attend social festivals. Now, in Decentraland, which has a maximum land class of 40,000, it will not be significant. We should think on a much larger scale. How Could everybody have something where the land gives them some sort of value, but also creates some sort of social involvement? We should look at something where virtual land has separate entertainment that we go to.

CRYPTO HIPSTER: I am thinking about two movies: *The Matrix* and *Total Recall*. You mentioned something earlier; you said Digital Disneyland. How could these metaverses not only be a place for entertainment, but for learning about topics like blockchain ethics, governance, or equal opportunities?

Michael: Well, with the most recent virtual reality we do, we just put these pieces together and hope that it manifests into actual virtual reality. We have a sense of presence that is just exploding under the surface. The Oculus Quest 2 is expected to sell about ten million headsets and it is about to become the default. If you log into Oculus Quest, you see some of the most popular games, or these kinds of social spaces. There are many people who flow into these virtual worlds. But a proper driver of future growth could be ethics. I suppose we should not overthink ethics too much right now. Let people have their fun, make their mistakes, run around, break their legs, and then put in some rules, but just the enormous potential ethical issues. We can consider I mean, what if we have forty land plots in Decentraland, and they are all owned by 40-something year old white men? Is that design a

SOLD OUT IN FIFTEEN SECONDS

welcoming environment for women, for people of other ethnicities?

There is this potential for concentration where we might end up with things that the blockchain easily incorporates but might not match social equality. For democracy, you should have land ownership rights, or have a vote... things that are improved by using blockchain technology. But what if you have a situation where there are two billion people visiting Decentraland? And democracy is being assessed by the fourteen landowners. That is a potentially perverse form of democracy. The blockchain must incorporate some elements of democracy, some elements of voting. I do not want to deliver a class or a course on ethics. I could end up learning loads, but I also realize that my knowledge is limited to ethics based on just financial ethics.

So, people are asking, "What about in a virtual world? If everybody walks around, doesn't any kind of disability become invisible?" Things like this we

SOLD OUT IN FIFTEEN SECONDS

can go into deeply, including how people design their characters. Or what if there was a belief system where a quarter of a world said they just want to mingle in cafes in a certain quarter of the world, and male and female characters must mingle separately? And you might vote on this. The concept might be objectively fair, because people are voting, but there must be a policy or an authority. People are great when they get together, but what we need is the concept of democracy itself from an ethical perspective that not the entire world believes in. Children need some sort of central God character who can hard-fork shifting gas if things get bad. There was an episode of *The Simpsons* that I watched many years ago, where they polluted the world so much that they lifted a polluted Springfield, and just dropped it in another place. We need someone with that type of power to just say when things get bad enough, we need to hard-fork our physical world and be transported out of Springfield.

SOLD OUT IN FIFTEEN SECONDS

It is easy to tell yourself you can have a lot of fun debating what the metaverse world should look like, and maybe that is the phase that we should be in. We should think about forming groups to talk about these things like what is the perfect virtual world. What should an economy look like? What should exist in the metaverse? Should there be a universal basic income and what is the minimum payment that everybody gets? Should people have to work to receive entertainment? All those types of things. It seems like it could be a potentially fun time to debate. The most Irish Pub conversations occur around football matches, so it is a step up. A controversial one.

CRYPTO HIPSTER: What are some considerations we must make when doing non-financial investing? What should people think about?

Michael: The first step is to have a parallel real world and virtual world... retail land versus physical retail. Retail land has value because of football. Is

SOLD OUT IN FIFTEEN SECONDS

there any innate difference between virtual football and physical football? I do not know. There is no difference in the rules of the game so you can model the virtual after the real world. We do not need to waste a lot of time for no reason. We can use models that already exist. If football is your sport, in the metaverse, consider the fact that people may teleport. Your economic model then needs to have a variable for teleportation ability. It is the same thing with advertising where you can create value potential. There was a sale in The Sandbox last week. An actual platform was selling metaverse land for about one thousand euro for a 2x2 plot of land with three NFTs that you could use for character entities. Or you can buy the land and sell NFTs to event attendees. There were people paying five hundred euro apiece for character NFTs. What do you think your virtual giraffe is going to be worth in 10 years' time? Notice, there is no economy for virtual drops, unless you are setting up a zoo. And I say most zoos lose money. So, what is your plan?

SOLD OUT IN FIFTEEN SECONDS

We need not get carried away with some of these things. If the NFT is a cloak, or a tunic curve, or something designed in an NFT world, just treat it as standard disposable clothes. If it is a billboard, treat it as a billboard for advertising. It is worth something to a business because it can direct people to your business. If it is a plot of land, you can build something that will attract people, and earn money. You need to discount everything because the future successful metaverses are not the current successful metaverses. These are all things you can model.

The mistake of thinking about the things that are an awful investment in the real world may make sense in the metaverse or in an empty world. There is no rational reason a pair of pants is worth is worth a million in a virtual world if you can get it for five Euros in your local supermarkets. We have not seen the beginning of what is going to happen. We are still only in the phase of thinking of this as a hobby. You cannot imagine that some businesses within those worlds might float on a stock exchange within those worlds. And you could be in a virtual pub talking about a virtual stock on the virtual floor having a conversation about stock markets in the real world. We could imagine that type of evolution and all have some fundamental doubts about what is going on. We are just two years old but already have quite a horrific existence. It is fun to think about some of this, but also something bigger. Few people think about these ideas.

CRYPTO HIPSTER: There's room there to think. How can people find out more information about your work, what you do, and who you are?

Michael: Twitter. As I have my name like Michael with an M in the middle. Michael M Dowling is my Twitter handle. Or just type Dublin City University and my name pops up. If anyone wants to reach out for a conversation, we would be delighted. It is always great to have conversations about the metaverse. So do not feel any hesitation. We do not have to talk about finances.

SOLD OUT IN FIFTEEN SECONDS

Chapter 4— Money Sports, Decentralized Gaming, and the Building of a Brand-New Industry

J.D. Salbego, Founder, CEO, and Art Director of AnRKey X, a cutting edge DeFi based gaming and NFT platform protocol, is a global leader in DeFi and crypto, market influencer, speaker, published author, and internationally recognized subject matter expert. J.D. is a featured contributor on Cointelegraph.com, frequently gives media interviews, has been quoted by leading blockchain and crypto news sites, and regularly speaks at leading conferences around the world like the World Economic Forum, and many more... His work has been featured in Forbes, Business Insider, and Yahoo Finance, including being linked to boosting Japan's economy with blockchain.

SOLD OUT IN FIFTEEN SECONDS

His links:

https://twitter.com/JDSalbego

https://www.jdsalbego.com/

For more AnRKey X updates, please follow us on our Twitter, Telegram Community, Telegram News, Medium, Discord, and LinkedIn.

Original Interview Date: April 17, 2021
Original Interview Link: https://spotifyanchor-web.app.link/e/vbJYtqJxavb

CRYPTO HIPSTER: Today, I have the honor and pleasure of introducing J.D. Salbego. He is the Chief Executive Officer of AnRKey X. J.D., welcome.

J.D.: Hey, thanks for having me. Excited to be on here.

SOLD OUT IN FIFTEEN SECONDS

CRYPTO HIPSTER: What is your background? And is it a logical background for what you do now?

J.D.: I have been in crypto for over five years. And this company I just launched in October is more logical, potentially, than everything I did in crypto up to this point. I was born and raised in Los Angeles and went straight into the music and entertainment business at age 17. I was always into technology. My father was an aerospace engineer and worked on the Apollo moon mission with N.A.S.A. and some of the first nuclear reactor submarines. I did not go that far. He is way beyond me. I am not a CTO, but I have that ingrained in me and I started as a recording engineer in the music industry, became Snoop Dogg's first engineer, or head engineer when I was 21 years old. And that led to you know, what I want to do is to be a music producer, record label owner and all that stuff. I had a label with Warner Music Group, and I collaborated with global celebrities. Snoop Dogg all the way to Eminem to Jason Derulo to, you know,

SOLD OUT IN FIFTEEN SECONDS

Britney Spears, all that stuff and was a music producer. I was at a publishing company and got into film and TV producing shows with NBC.

Then I got into crypto about five plus years ago. I spent 17 years in music entertainment before I got into crypto just because I was obsessed with it. And I got a few calls after advising a bunch of companies and networking. A lot of the major initial people that launched it, or I would say around 2013 and 2014, Brock Pierce and the whole DNA were in Santa Monica, while I was in Los Angeles. I grew up hanging around them and that is how I started networking. I got some calls and it launched my career in crypto overnight. An overnight success and I went straight into, funny enough, investment banking. I was advising Initial Coin Offerings. I became the face of a lot of companies as an executive because I had a successful record quickly for raising capital, advising ICOs, going to market, big communication strategies, and helping companies both in the U.S. and in Asia expand. I

SOLD OUT IN FIFTEEN SECONDS

became the American Asian expert, and even helped Mike Novogratz when he launched Galaxy Digital early on. He set his first office up in Tokyo, and I helped him expand there. Same thing with DNA Fund. I help them expand in Asia too, and a lot of other companies.

I was the CEO of a crypto exchange in Singapore. And I launched this company AnRKey X, which merges decentralized finance (DeFi) based financial products liquidity and mining, then gamifies it with eSports. And then some unique NFT models into a gaming platform, which we call gDEX, a DeFi gaming platform exchange. I was back in the creative world. I am the art director too. So even though our team is phenomenal, we worked on Final Fantasy, and you name it, some of the biggest game companies. You know our CTO is ex Morgan Stanley. I started at Goldman Sachs. Every NFT, you see the game designs are all me. I have designed it or I started the concepts and left it to all our teams.

SOLD OUT IN FIFTEEN SECONDS

So, I am back in the creative world. So that is why it is more logical, and hence why I am wearing a t-shirt, and not a sports coat and a tight collar, as you see in most of my stuff online, because that is what I was doing. I was interviewed at Bloomberg and at NASDAQ. The World Economic Forum had me speak. I was a public speaker in crypto for the past year and spoke by about thirty of the biggest policies and now get to run my company as CEO and the creative guy. And it is fun. I wear a t-shirt.

CRYPTO HIPSTER: What inspired you to create AnRKey X?

J.D.: I was working on solutions. Honestly, I had no intention of getting back into business writing technology. And we are dealing with liquidity mining, farming, staking, and decentralized buyers. We deal with clients, but it is highly creative. If you look at all our online properties or game designs or NFTs that have been selling out, hitting number one, back-to-back to back-to-back on wearables. It

SOLD OUT IN FIFTEEN SECONDS

is creative. I did not plan for this at all. I am hugely into spirituality and synchronicity. Carl Jung coined that term back in the 1930s or 1940s. It has been written in every school philosophy, and it is a very spiritual moment for me. I came full circle back to the creative stuff. Even producing music again, which is crazy. And what I saw last year, as I was running the exchange, was liquidity mining had just blown up. Uniswap is genius, right? The algorithms and the financial models behind automated market making and these liquidity pools, phenomenal. Then someone created the farming compound. Suddenly, you had this whole farming as an inception model. It never ends. You can just keep taking an LP token, going here, and going there. And it was just a tremendous boom. I was fascinated by it. I was like, there is no use case in farming at all. But there is with gDEX. I just started seeing a lot of trends happening there. Boom!

I was really fascinated by it. And I have always been fascinated by video games and social

SOLD OUT IN FIFTEEN SECONDS

entertainment. I am an entertainment guy. I have been for my whole life. For 17 years, I was in entertainment. And I started seeing like, well, there are some use cases, and thought about how we can build out a use case for farming. Obviously, we see that with ATMs, the unit swaps. There is a use case there. But how can we really do this whole decentralized finance movement in the farming aspect? How can we build a sustainable use case for gamification?

I really started seeing these trends; I hired an analyst; we sat in all the sizeable communities of the Uniswap compound and all the new ones like Base Money. I have always loved Base Money because they are so creative. They are weird memes and gifts. The philosophy behind what their stuff is, it is more than amazingly simple farming stuff. They talk about money. If you really look at what their philosophy is that money is meaningless. If you really get into their background, people have authored articles about it. Pretty influential people too, just to validate my thoughts. It is interesting as a science experiment. Go sit in Base Money as a science experience and look at what they talk about, how they talk to their users, and what their users say. The experiential meanings behind the memes and stuff that they use in the content I had been fascinated with, like a social experiment.

In high school, I thought I wanted to be a neuroscientist. That was really my goal at one point. Therefore, I wanted to do a cross study if my whole life was going to be about neuroscience, quantum physics, and philosophy, because I am still super nerdy. I studied biological psychology for two years when I was in high school. I was fascinated, but then I realized, like, I have not gone to school for 10 years. No way. And I did not want to become a therapist, sitting around for eight hours daily and other people's problems. I do that enough with my family. I am Italian and Latin. There's always drama in our types of families. I kept that stuff as a hobby. But the point being, I was fascinated by the

SOLD OUT IN FIFTEEN SECONDS

psychology of the crypto community with this decentralized finance. It is a new breed of people. It is a new consumer profile. These people, mixed with the Covid lockdowns and the new online commerce, I found fascinating. I started seeing the gamification of how you can build use cases. I also, through that time, started really seeing how everyone is doing eSports right now. That is what we got. Everyone is doing these communities for financial products.

And then boom, a month or two ago, GameStop hit and Wall Street Bets, and what we do is terribly similar. It is completely legal too. What they were doing was not legal, just to be noticeably clear. But you see exactly what happened with Wall Street Bets. You will see there is a pinnacle moment in 2000. Now, you will see where the world is headed, and why video games now, globally, are a bigger market than the global movie business and the United States sports industries combined. That tells you a lot. We are at a boom right now. Innovative technology, new products, new digital experiences. We are in a movement. As you can tell, there is something happening right now.

CRYPTO HIPSTER: How do you compare the 1920s in the U.S. the movie industry and all the social stuff? And how do you see the back-alley bars and stuff like that compared to the eSports movement?

J.D.: If you are going to talk about back alley around the 1920s, you talk about bootlegging, too. And then you also talk about cons and gambling, as well. You see strategy within gambling; you see strategy with people breaking the law. Let us talk about that. If you really want to get there, I am pushing too far with bootlegging. Hence why the Kennedys had so much money, but I will not start that entire conversation.

I love how the world works. I find it fascinating. We are a herd-based species, which is what I see. We are human beings. I find it fascinating right now

SOLD OUT IN FIFTEEN SECONDS

where we are. I truly do. With NFTs, I really was always fascinated with them, but thought there was no scalability. They had no real economic supply and demand when they first blew up. What I focused on with our company was creating what we call a proprietary NFT engine that we used to derive a base value model to price our NFTs. All our NFTs produce yield. In our games, we have four different models, so even our collectibles that we are selling, our variables can be staked in live game action in our liquidity gamified liquidity mining eSports game. And then we have three other types of models that all look like video games, and are things you can do, such as boosting a weapon purchase to make them explode. That is a one-person shooter mini game like spaceships. It is cool, futuristic, and has never been done before. It is all based on the team base component. It is all based on generating the highest aggregate yield between your teams, with the winner earning the prize pool.

SOLD OUT IN FIFTEEN SECONDS

CRYPTO HIPSTER: I grew up, you know, playing Space Invaders and Pac Man on Atari. You described AnRKey X acts as traditional gaming. Or pinball meets DeFi and eSports. How do these new cryptos in this gaming realm intersect with the traditional gaming?

J.D.: There's several ways to answer that. The first use case of blockchain was in gaming back in 2002. And the reason was because the easiest use case to adopt was digital assets in video games that were being transferred around between users. The next biggest use case was financial products. That was the easiest one, but there was also a lot of friction because the government knew what we were doing and they did not like it. Traditional gamers love to spend their time driving value out of competitions, achieving goals, experiencing things, and collaborating with friends and teams. Also, they love to purchase valuable digital assets and trade them in the game. How that compares with us is this is the first time you can get paid to play games the same way. You can have the same experience and earn money in our game. It is unique. It is the first time because we based our NFT engine, and our entire game on this derivative-based value model. It is a fully incentivized community right to play these games, because the more they play these games, the more money they earn, and the more valuable the assets inside grow. Our utility token works to get arcade coins, but within our economic models in the generation of API through endgame actions. That creates the price value, and the API is based on a fiat model. If you really look at the supply and demand cost of goods, multiple parties agree on something, except ours is not run by the government. Ours is private and is fully public on the blockchain. And completely real and transparent.

CRYPTO HIPSTER: What lessons do you think we can take from your games? And then how does that apply to the entertainment sector? And then any other sectors where they are trying to have massive migration and adoption of blockchain?

J.D.: That was a loaded question. There are about four components to that. I mean, obviously I do not believe NFTs are for money laundering. We can go down that rabbit hole with crypto versus cash, and what the Federal Reserve and our governments did in 2008, and then discuss how HSBC and every other bank launder trillions of U.S. Dollars. We will not go down THAT rabbit hole.

The basis of the NFT technology is absolutely mind blowing from a principle that you can create a unique digital asset. You know, that is the difference between a fungible and a nonfungible token. Bitcoin is a fungible token. Bitcoins are not unique. Ethereum tokens are not unique. But a nonfungible token has a unique code for each one. So that can be applied not only to the gaming industry, but to any industry. If you see the future of blockchain, which is the next stage of innovation

SOLD OUT IN FIFTEEN SECONDS

and Web 3.0, you will have legal agreements, lawyers, data, and everything beyond the blockchain. The question becomes how you capture multiple drafts of a legal agreement on the blockchain. How do you do that with a nonfungible token? How do you make unique copies of one thing to distribute all your files on the blockchain? What do you mean you have to tokenize each file?

If you only tokenize the blockchain and these contracts using a fungible token, the basis of these files will not be unique. To make different drafts of that legal agreement to the final clean one that has been signed, make a nonfungible version of it, then they are all unique. That is how genius NFTs are. The other genius thing is with smart contracts. You can sell them and put a price in there, what you want to be paid out in a secondary market. And then say, Okay, I am going to sell this for $1, every time after it gets sold you want 10% of that, because I am the creator and want royalty income. Well, every time it gets sold on the secondary market, with no middleman, no interference, completely automated, completely transparent, completely public completely distributed across the ledger, immutable, that transaction automatically gets sends a portion of that right back to your wallet. We are talking about Star Wars right now with no human interference, no SWIFT, no transfer agent, no nothing. That is how this relates to the rest of the world within our games. Just by having NF T's we can now buy, sell, and trade and hold, hold a digital asset and transfer it across the web. Now, that is the genius of it. NFT's are in the technology's genius.

CRYPTO HIPSTER: In 2018, I had a consulting client. It was a patent troll company where they have a general portfolio and have extremely specific patents that go under each of their portfolios. And I recommended Crypto Kitties (ERC-721) to them. And their lawyers had a fit. How far have we come since Crypto Kitties then to now? What have been the improvements or the breakthroughs since then?

SOLD OUT IN FIFTEEN SECONDS

J.D.: There has not been that much improvement in Ethereum at all because we have scalability issues. The new improvements with Layer One are stuck. Luckily, we have Layer Two now, with which we are partnering. We partner with the creators of Layer Two, which are called Polygon, formerly MATIC. Coinbase, who invests in them, just listed them. Polygon helps build our games and they are part of our team. The Layer Two protocol reduces gas fees down to almost zero. While Layer One of Ethereum has not changed since Crypto Kitties, what has changed is the innovation behind NFTs.

We were one of the first movers in the decentralized finance/NFT/gaming movement. That is why we started the DeFi gaming coalition with Polygon, along with the biggest security auditing firms and the biggest other DeFi companies as well. We see the innovation people are doing. This innovation includes unique things with NFT's, from staking them for collateral, or using them with in-game assets to generate yield and unlock many utilities.

SOLD OUT IN FIFTEEN SECONDS

People are yield-farming with NFTs and that is groundbreaking, crazy, and unique stuff. That is where I see the innovation going, is that there's tons of companies and projects and people really trying to innovate the NFTs. Technology will catch up soon. Layer two is being mass adopted within our industry, and there is only one Level Two marketplace right now. And we use them for our APIs. There is only one URL to Open Sea and you can look at it right now in beta. It is still taking a while. Once we cross that paradigm, it will be incredible.

Our NFT collectibles tell you the different models are like Pokemon cards that have been game applied to DeFi. We do not really auction our game cards off. These mass adoption game cards are cheap. Everyone can buy them. They range from $50 to $400. Just like video games, we want mass adoption. We just dropped the first one a little over a month ago and since then, we have generated almost $800,000 in sales just from our collectibles.

SOLD OUT IN FIFTEEN SECONDS

Before partnering with Polygon, Ethereum gas was so high that people were paying $180 in gas fees just to purchase one of our cards that cost $350. While we are flattered, the demand was so high, the problem with Ethereum is the network is still getting clogged. Our page even shut down and you could see the server went down too. Luckily, the innovation of companies like us and Polygon enable us to do unique things. The adoption with the industry still needs to kick up a notch right now.

CRYPTO HIPSTER: What are your thoughts on how your relationship with Polygon is going that will help reduce Ethereum fees?

J.D.: It is phenomenal. Those guys created Level Two. Our game is full Layer Two right now. It is like a million transactions for ten cents. You hear that number of a million transactions for ten cents. I just told you one Ethereum transaction costs $180, plus it gets clogged. Our relationship with Polygon is phenomenal. You know, we talk to them every day.

SOLD OUT IN FIFTEEN SECONDS

Every day we have business marketing chats with them. They work with our games through a developer chat. We connect them in the ecosystem; they connect us to theirs. They are incredibly supportive. They just built a great protocol and they are heavily pushing the community and bringing companies like ours together. They have connected us with brilliant companies to partner, we connect with them. And we all just build this industry together because there is enough business consumers and revenue to go around. There is no greed here. We are all excited to build this and to be the first people to build something so unique in the industry. I am American. I want to make money, of course. And I must make money for investors and people but get to work on stuff that has never been done before. To me, that is unique, fun, and exciting.

CRYPTO HIPSTER: Do you bring up the community? The community overall has taken a hit this past year plus with COVID-19. As we move and migrate toward a post-COVID world, how do you see the evolution of e-gaming? Where do you see that direction headed?

J.D.: That's an interesting question. Where do we go after COVID? What is the world going to be like? I do not think it is going to regress. I think we have just merged. We were already there. Spending more time online now is just sped up to us. The reason gaming is so big and has grown our industry through decentralized finance, and all these other things, and NFTs are because of COVID. We are just going to continue to be driven by more online experiences.

Gaming has become increasingly online, but it is now sectors of gaming styles, ecosystems and communities within gaming and eSports that are being generated. There is a gamification of every industry now. Like the supply chain, through financial products, trading, online, social entertainment, everything is becoming gamified right now with NFTs. Blockchain is the future.

Web 2.0 could not solve the transfer of value. You have a double spending problem with money, hence why there's SWIFT transfer agents. And then digital assets are completely replicated under Web 2.0.

Web 3.0 and blockchain technology changes all that. And now, as you spend more time online, we now have figured out a way, especially with NFTs to safeguard the value and the right to generate and protect that value, to trade, to earn margin on that value, with no human interference. It is all peer-to-peer. What that does is create a new ecosystem, additional revenue streams, and new opportunities for people to get creative and just make anything. I come from Hollywood and in that background so we were launching in about two to three weeks would be a huge media push throughout our industry and in Hollywood we are launching a new purely celebrity driven marketplace. We already

SOLD OUT IN FIFTEEN SECONDS

have about seven celebrities, including some who we call icons, such as a famous singer and basketball player. We are taking branded value right the celebrities because there is a collectible aspect in there that's not just random artists who have not established themselves yet. These celebrities can generate revenue from art and have a mass following. That is how you generate value.

With a celebrity brand a collectible, this digital thing has value now. We are wrapping many components into this and working on some unique stuff. Just watch our channels over the next three weeks to four weeks, and you will start seeing some amazing things happening with celebrities. We launched it under AnRKey X.

CRYPTO HIPSTER: How do you see the prediction markets playing into the NFTs to create forecasts and prediction NFTs that you never saw before?

SOLD OUT IN FIFTEEN SECONDS

J.D.: I think is incredible. If you look at our roadmap, we have that for our second quarter to build out our prediction market within our games. You ought to launch a prediction market with NFTs. I have seen companies getting that is where it is going to go. You can make a prediction market anywhere and people have a right in the traditional world with gambling, with stocks, and with NFTs, where you could predict anything. It is fun that you can make money from it. It is gamification, and it is going to happen soon, once there are enough assets out there that the secondary market is big enough. Within our game, we have some new stuff within our price and where we can do it without being tied to someone else's ecosystem, or some other market being developed first. Prediction markets are the future because they work great in every industry already.

CRYPTO HIPSTER: Thank you. I appreciate your time today. How can people find out more

SOLD OUT IN FIFTEEN SECONDS

information about your products or services and contact you if they want?

J.D.: Just go to our website. All our socials and our entire community are there. That is spelled anrkeyx.io. That is the same thing for our Twitter. I am J.D. Salbego on Twitter, or jdsalbego.com. And that is our easiest way to find what we do. We are regularly active in our community. Things are going fantastically. We are super grateful. We have been working, slaving away 24/7 for six months now. Thank you for having me. It was fun.

Appendix A: About the Author

Jamil Hasan

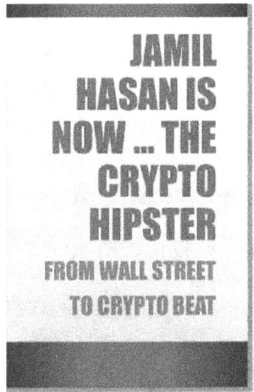
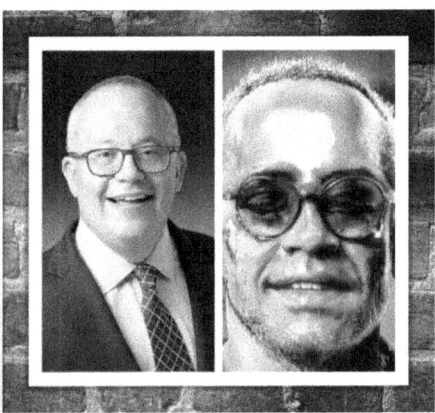

Born in 1971 - 51 Years old

Master's Degree in Finance, from Drexel University

Bachelor's Degree in Liberal Arts from Virginia Tech

https://www.linkedin.com/in/jamil-hasan-63bb71

Certified Digital Asset Advisor, from PlannerDAO

Certified Digital Asset Professional, from Global Digital Asset and Cryptocurrency Association

Areas of expertise: Crypto/Blockchain, NFTs/Metaverse, Writing/Editing, Podcasting/Interviewing, Insurance and Investments, Coaching/Speaking, Finance and Technology Project Management, Leadership

Values: Jamil is a visionary and resilient thought leader who believes in empathy, integrity, ethics, and compassion as core values in everything he does. He entered the cryptocurrency space in 2017 to help make the world a better place by giving the power of money to the people through decentralization ... and to help Generation X have a voice in the decentralized economy, a voice Jamil feels was not considered when the new financial laws in the U.S.A. were written under the Dodd Frank Act. (For more information about this topic, please read Jamil's book **Re-Generation X: How Generation X Can Leverage Blockchain Technology to Save Themselves and Rebuild America).**

The Crypto Hipster Podcast

Jamil is the founder of Crypto Hipster Publications LLC, and the Crypto Hipster Podcast, where he has interviewed entrepreneurs, founders, executives and artists globally in crypto and blockchain. He has built three shows: The Crypto Hipster Podcast, Crypto Hipster's Chronicles, and the X-Factor with the Crypto Hipster. He has an active listener audience across six continents. The podcasts can be found at anchor.fm/crypto-hipster-podcast.

Blockchain Ethics

Proven Leadership – Jamil coined the phrase "Blockchain Ethics" and has written three compelling books on the subject, arguing in favor of blockchain's bright future and dispelling false narratives surrounding the true value of decentralized economies.

Corporate and Entrepreneurial History

Jamil spent eighteen years working on Wall Street, including eleven years at American International Group, Inc., where he built data departments and information engines across operations, finance, and technology divisions in the investments, life insurance and property/casualty business lines. In 2017, Jamil left Wall Street and joined the Blockchain and Crypto Revolutions to help bring justice and equality in areas of the economy where they are needed most.

Content Portfolio and Media Appearances

Jamil has hosted over 190 podcasts and has also been guest in mainstream media, youtube channels, and podcasts, speaking about blockchain and cryptocurrencies. The content topics Jamil has hosted and spoken about cover a wide range of global issues.

SOLD OUT IN FIFTEEN SECONDS

Appendix B: Crypto Hipster Podcasts

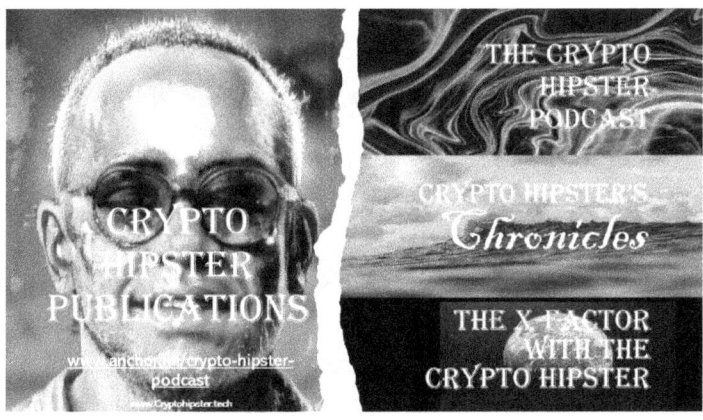

A complete list of Jamil's Crypto Hipster Podcasts is presented below. All of them can be found at anchor.fm/crypto-hipster-podcast and can be listened to on Spotify, Apple Podcasts, Amazon, Anchor, or wherever enjoy your favorite podcasts, including the full interviews from each of the guests presented in this book.

Bitcoin

- Bitcoin Lessons from El Salvador and Onboarding New Crypto Users within Seconds, Geoff McCabe, Divi Project
- Building efficient data centers, environmental sustainability, and eco-friendly power grids with Bitcoin mining, with Tad Piper and ComputeNorth
- Building New, Clean, and Sustainable Energy Sources with Bitcoin, Idealism, and Intelligent Mining, Daniel Elimelech
- Crypto trends to watch in 2022 and beyond with Caroline Bowler, BTC Markets, CEO, Blockchain Australia
- Earning Bitcoin by Shopping Your Favorite Brands, and the Future of Crypto Mergers and Acquisitions, with Alex Adelman and Lolli
- From fiat to Bitcoin, the transition of analog to digital, Matt Senter, Lolli

SOLD OUT IN FIFTEEN SECONDS

- How Entrepreneurs, Open Governments, and Female Shoppers Could Fuel a $10 Million Bitcoin Price by 2030, with Tim Draper
- Nuclear Fusion, Lightning, and Sovereignty with Bitcoin Mining and Romain Nouzareth and CCU
- Satoshi's Vision, Hybridization, and the Great Centralized Compromise with Nick Saponaro at The Divi Project
- The importance of Carbon Neutrality with Arthur Lee, SAI Tech
- The latest Bitcoin Insights, including Taproot, Lightning Network News, and Inflation, with Peter Nagle at Bitcove
- What are Bitcoin's biggest concerns in 2021, insights with Matthew Le Merle, Managing Partner of Blockchain Coinvestors
- What the World Could be like IF Bitcoin BSV were the Real Bitcoin, Richard Boase, Satoshi Block Dojo

- Why all American banks are talking about bitcoin, the challenges of markets, exchanges and digitising assets with Michael Creadon, Inveniam
- Why Bitcoin? Because ... Venezuela. A personal account of the impact of hyperinflation
- Why Economists are Often Wrong about Bitcoin, David Palmer, Vodafone

Crypto's Future

- 400 Deaths and an Explosion in Private Market Crypto Valuations as Wall Street is eaten by Bitcoin
- Achieving the U.N. Sustainable Health and Food Goals with Food and Health Data Aggregator Esca, Shalom Osiadi
- Are We Misunderstanding Blockchain's Potential or Headed for Crypto Winter 2.0? with David Long, CVVC

- Block Kong: The Current Crypto Scene in Hong Kong and China's CBDC Status with Charles d'Haussy
- Creating a Crypto Carbon Credit Index with Regenerative Tokenomics, Demian Klenk
- Crypto trends to watch for 2022, David Schwartz, Director, Litecoin Foundation
- Future-Proofing, Scaling, and Building Interoperable Networks Are Not That Far Away ... They Are Just Beyond the Horizon, with Rob Viglione @ Horizen Labs
- How to Identify Crypto Opportunities, Richard Carthon, Crypto Current
- How to succeed in Crypto and the Blockchain Industry, Ryan Williams, The Blockchain Academy
- Legacy Tokens, ESG Investing and Solving Greenwashing with Nature's Vault, Phil Rickard
- Leveraging AI and Machine Learning with Matt Dixon, EVAI

- Leveraging the Power of Communities to Create Sustainable City-Driven Utility-Token Economies, with Intercoin and Greg Magarshak
- Old Paradigms Die Hard: Shifting from the Analog to the Digital Blockchain Economy, Don Tapscott
- Surviving the PayPal Wars and crypto insights with Eric Jackson, PayPal Mafia, TransitNet and more
- Understanding the Rise of Technosocialism, with author Brett King
- What you need to know about the future of Cryptocurrencies and the digital Euro with Sean Brizendine, SecureX
- Why Blockchain is for Everyone, insights with Sir John Hargrave
- Why Wall Street is Running Scared of Inclusive Capitalism
- The Race Against an Orwellian Future is ON. Let's Go!!, with Geoff McCabe @ LetsGo

- The Role of Faith-Based Cryptocurrencies and the Power of Dominion, with Gregory Jones and NASDAC Crypto Coin

Decentralized Autonomous Organizations

- Building an educational DAO with Blockchain at Berkeley co-founder Jon Allen
- Stem-Cell Breakthroughs and the Regenerative Birth of Jimmy's Justice DAO, James Ryan
- Using On-Chain Analytics and Social Sentiment Data To Leverage Artificial Intelligence, DAO Marcello Mari
- Wyoming setting a new precedent with crypto friendly legislation and Decentralized Autonomous Organizations, with Ori Shimony

Decentralized Finance

- $1B in assets managed by the Kava software, Brian Kerr, CEO, Kava Labs explains more
- Bridging Traditional and Decentralized Finance Industries with Data Tunnels, Matthijs de Vries, AllianceBlock
- Building resilience in the Internet of Things, Decentralized Finance, Banking and Mobility with the IOTA Foundation, with Dan Simerman
- Building Smart MultiSig Wallets for Institutional DeFi Adoption, Christopher McGregor
- Building the decentralized global blockchain infrastructure on TRON, with TRON DAO
- Building the Internet Computer, Web 3.0 Liz Yang, DFINITY Foundation
- Cloudmoney: Cash, Cards, Crypto, and the War for Our Wallets, an interview with author Brett Scott

- Creating a decentralized, patient-centric, data-driven healthcare economy and network to empower patients globally, with Pradeep Goel and Solve.Care
- Creating a Thriving Self Sovereign Identity through Privacy and Thrivacy Wallet, Dr Gordon Jones
- Creating Crypto Lending Solutions for Institutions, DeFi's impact on Banks, and the Future of Finance with Howard Krieger and UnFederalReserve
- Creating Efficiencies in Banking and Politics with Hybrid Decentralized Finance with Pedro Torres @ Roseon.FinancePedro Torres is the Co-founder and Head of Quant at Roseon.Finance
- Defying the Traditional Trends by Helping Investors Make Confident Crypto Decisions with Imgesu Cetin
- Exploiting Nudge Economics and Blockchain Technology to Disrupt the $200 Billion Rewards Points Industry

SOLD OUT IN FIFTEEN SECONDS

- From Financial Markets to Decentralized Leveraged Markets, with Vaibhav Kadikar, CloseCross
- How to predict rug pulls when making crypto investments and donations Nick Smart
- How to Review and Rate Decentralized Finance (DeFi) Protocols with Rex Hygate at DeFi Safety
- How to set up a crypto Cayman fund and a crypto license in Lithuania
- How to Solve the Oracle Dilemma and Entropy using SupraOracles, with Joshua Tobkin34:061310Published5/7/22
- Mitigating Crypto Control Risks and What Future Banks and DeFi Products Look Like for Investors, with Philipp Pieper and Swarm Markets
- The challenges of driving crypto adoption, Rosario Ingargiola, Bosonic Digital
- The importance of Financial Smart Contracts, Ralf Kubli, Casper Association

- The Importance of Technology Investing for Women, Angelika Dehmel, BUX
- The Intersection of Social, Economic and Technology Advancements with a Developer Blockchain Toolkit
- Transfer Agency and Japanese Banking, with Jamie Finn, Co-Founder at Securitize
- Transfer Agency as a "Good Control Location" for Cryptocurrencies, Scott Harrigan
- Transitioning from Traditional Finance to Decentralized Finance : Creating and Building DeFi products and protocols with Bifrost

Blockchain Ethics

- A Brave New World: The Power of Building an Altruistic Global Society, with Fran Strajnar

SOLD OUT IN FIFTEEN SECONDS

- A Father's Journey to Humanity; and a Criminal Complaint to the U.S. Department of Justice, with James Ryan @ Omgeneum
- Blockchain for Good, Helen Hai, United Nations Goodwill Ambassador for Industrialization in Africa
- Building an Ethical Hedge and Thoughts on Charlie Lee and Elon Musk with Litecoin Foundation Director David Schwartz
- Inspiring Digital futures in Afghanistan for women, Fereshteh Forough Code to Inspire
- Lessons from the Bitfinex Hack and Mars Stealer Malware Threats, Justin Choo, Cabital
- The importance of Blockchain Ethics with David Kay, Liti Capital
- Using Blockchain to Reunite Families, Kristine Smith
- A Father's Journey for Humanity; and a Criminal Complaint to the U.S. Department of Justice, with James Ryan @ Omgeneum

Gaming

- Betting Big on In-Game Fantasy Sports Betting and the Future of Rugby, Paddy Power
- Building Gaming Communities with WAX and Blockchain Brawlers, Michael Rubinelli
- E-sports, Decentralized Gaming, and the Building of a brand new industry: Money Sports, with J.D. Salbego and AnRKey X
- How to build a blockchain gaming platform, Gregory Crous, H3RO3S
- How to navigate global gaming challenges, Don Norbury, Shrapnel
- NFT gaming trends to watch with Ishan NegiIshan, Polygon Studios
- The Impact of Covid on the Future of eSports and Live Gaming, with Joseph Chong and the League of Ancients
- Verge Crypto, Quantum, Casino Coins, and Cyber Insights with Mark Wittenberg and Mihael Radoslovic

- Virtual Reality Gaming, Crypto Insights from Miami, Jonathan Ovadia, AEXLab

Leadership

- Betting Your Future with Conviction in BolieCoin, with Craig Curtis
- Bitcoin, ten years on the roller coaster, and where it may go next, insights with crypto legend Charlie Shrem
- Blockchain, Pandemics, and Utility Tokens from the Founder of Fortitude Ranch, Dr. Drew Miller
- Building a Collaborative Decentralized Society through Servant Leadership, Cyrus Taghehchian, CEO, Splyt Core Foundation
- Building a Resilient Skill Set for the Decentralized Economy, with Leigh Cuen
- Creating healthy ecosystems and a sustainable future with Sebnem Rusitschka, Crypto Token Flower

- How algorithmic search applications can help in finance, Meir Shachar, Powerlinx
- How Building a Data-Driven Health-Focused Organization During the Coronavirus Pandemic Won the Admiration and Support of the National Science Foundation and the Blockchain Industry, with Susan Joseph
- How street smarts and thinking on your feet can take you a long, long way: tech & crypto insights with Monty Munford, Sienna Network
- How the PadawanDAO can help students to go to blockchain conferences Eason Wu, TKS
- Innovation insights with Samaira Mehta, a 13 year old TIME Young Leader Shaping the Decade
- Rolling with the Punches: How JUSTTIP is transforming the service sector for tipped employees in Ireland
- The Knowledge Society, Creating Global Social and Economic Reform, Navid Nathoo

- The Roles of Existentialism, Nihilism, and Nondualism in Emerging Technologies, Blockchain and Quantum Computing
- Using Blockchain to achieve Global Social Impact, Samantha Ouyang

Metaverses

- Building a Better Metaverse with Better Architecture, with Tomas Zacek
- Building the Infrastructure for Decentralized Identity within the Metaverse, Enjin Rene Stefancic
- Building the metaverse city of Lobsteropolis - the future of lobsters as sentient and metaversal beings.
- Building the Metaverse, insights with Simon Kertonegoro, My Metaverse
- Building the world's premier luxury branded metaverse mall
- Live from Davos, Switzerland, global leader in cryptocurrencies, Felix Honigwachs

- Navigating Your Hyper-Real Synthetic Likeness in the Metaverse with Deep Fakes, Tom Graham
- NFTs and Building the Metaverse with Jamie Goldblatt and Mind Chill 360 Media
- Real Estate Development Opportunities in the Metaverse, Erin Sykes
- Staying Safe in the Metaverse and the Private Key Paradox, Ruben Merre
- Stepping into the Metaverse: Building Digital DisneyLand with Michael Dowling, Finance Professor at Dublin City University
- The challenges of building a metaverse entertainment platform, insights with Colin Fitzpatrick, Animal Concerts.
- The value of Industrially Designed 3-Dimensional Metaverse Marketplaces, insights with Julian Picaza, SmartMFG
- Using the Metaverse to Transform Logistics, Sandeep Aggarwal, Logix

- Creating Metaverse Experiences, Leaving a Legacy, and Bringing Tupac Back to Life, with Justin Trevor Winters @ Verified Labs

Mobility

- Achieving Sustainability in Fleet Management with a Unique Electrical Vehicle Data Approach, with Geotab and David Savage
- Building a Scooter-Based Eco-Friendly Transportation Infrastructure as Mobility Done Right, with Charlie Gleeson and Zipp Mobility

Non-Fungible Tokens

- A Brand New World of BioDiversity and Wild Animal Conservation with Wild Earth NFT
- Building a Blueprint for Trust, Thoughts on Spencer Dinwiddie and The Role of Hedera

Hashgraph in Blockchain Governance, with Dr. Leemon Baird
- Building an NFT Marketplace for Global Healthcare, Dr. Michael J Kaldasch, Almedis Blockchain
- Building Communities through NFTs, with Matt Street, Lucky Maneki NFT
- Conducting Early Stage Market Validation and Building No-Code Storefronts for NFTs and Web 3.0
- Creating art and smart rings from microbes and biology-based NFTs, David Kvitsiani, CNICK
- Crypto from the Red Carpet: Celebrity NFT and Metaverse Insights with Entertainment Producer Sophie Watts
- Empowering Women and creating Fair Labor in the Fashion Supply Chain, Lindsey Mallon
- Gardening and Sculpture NFTs can create a healthy mindset, Ken Folan, Kildare Gallery

SOLD OUT IN FIFTEEN SECONDS

- How Abstract Artists can Start to Create NFTs on OpenSea and use them for Philanthropy
- How Cannabis and Crypto are Helping This Artist Survive Terminal Cancer, with Arabella Proffer
- How more women can become involved in NFTs, Sara Nemati, artist and contributor Bored Ape Ladies NFT collective
- How Tapping into Our Creativity and Memories can Eradicate Toxic Happiness and Improve Mental Health
- How to Create Limited Edition NFTs with Amelia Tomasicchio at the Cryptonomist
- How to earn Royalties with Lithographic Prints using Zero Knowledge Proofs, with TreeTrunk and John Wolpert
- How to rate Celebrity NFTs, insights with Joey Dunne, aka LeDrop WithCheese

SOLD OUT IN FIFTEEN SECONDS

- Incorporating Cutting-Edge Digital Technologies while Building Digital Production Systems, Dilek Sezen, TreeTrunk
- Indexing, Swapping, and Aggregating Non Fungible Tokens, with Ori Levi and NFTrade
- Initial NFT Offerings with Steve Good and Dreams Quest
- Ksoids, Orangutans, and the Opportunity to Impact Our Global Carbon Footprint with NFTs, with Danil Kviroruchko and Andy Alexhin
- NFTs for dummies, art, investments, crypto punks and more all explained with Jamil Hasan & Jillian Godsil
- Painting the Invisible - How Artists and Scientists are paving the path for NFTs in film and painting with Christian Hook
- Repurposing AK47s for peace, CRYPTO KALASH stories with Bran Symondson
- Reshaping the Diamond Industry with Consortiums, NFTs, and Blockchained

Supply Chains with Diamante Blockchain and Chirag Jetani
- Retro Cat NFTs, Korean inspirations with artist Stephanie Ishler
- SHABANG!!: Discovering your inner NFT with world famous photographer Peter Hurley
- Sold Out in 15 Seconds: How Graffiti Kings and Street Art are Capturing the NFT Art World's Attention and Trust, Darren Cullen aka SER
- Squirrel Syndrome: Why chasing 'Bright and Shiny' in Gaming NFTs often leaves investors and gamers empty handed, Jawad Ashraf
- The Collector's Dilemma, Role of Crypto Experts, and the Intersection of NFTs and Blockchain Innovation with Sarina Charugundla
- The duality of life as half man, half cyborg, crypto and NFT insights with collective conscious artist Orrin

SOLD OUT IN FIFTEEN SECONDS

- The NFT Handbook - Obtaining a Comprehensive Overview of the Global NFT Market with QuHarrison Terry
- The Role of Enthusiasm and the Importance of Winning in Crypto With Tally Founder, Dennison Bertram
- What NFT Life is Like as an Original CryptoPunk
- Why NFT Birds are better than Punks, Apes and Horses, with Daniel Steeves and tudaBirds
- Building a Nifty, Resurgent Web 3.0 Movement for NFT Content Creators, with the Nexus Voyagers' Network, with Ben and Miles
- Making NFT & Cryptocurrency Part of Mainstream Everyday Life, with Julian Rodriguez @ Momento NFT

Public Relations / Marketing

- A better future for online content and streaming in a post Youtube world with Jeremy Kauffman, Founder LBRY, Odysee
- B2B and Healthcare Insights and the Role of Influence in Social Media, with Evan Kirstel
- How to do PR right in the Crypto world, Armel Leslie, Peaks Strategies
- Mining Website Traffic and Social Media to Build Publishers' Internet Presence, Reggie Jerath, Gather
- What to Look Forward to the Most During Istanbul Blockchain Week, with Erhan Korhaliller
- Why crypto adoption is coming sooner than you think, Michael Casey, CoinDesk

Regulatory Frameworks

- Alleviating Data Protection Risks with Multi-Party Computation and Partisia Blockchain, Kurt Neilsen
- Challenges and Opportunities with Developing a Global Crypto Regulatory Framework, William Je
- Creating a Regulatory Framework for the Collaborative Decentralized World, with Li Jun, Founder of Ontology
- Decentralized Finance Yield, Regulatory Compliance, and Building Compliant Platforms, Raymond Hsu, Cabital.
- Security Tokens, Energy Tokenization and Regulatory Lessons from the Middle East, with Walid Abou Zaki
- Setting codes of conduct and best AML/KYC practices for the virtual assets, Malcolm Wright, Global Digital Finance

Space

- Not So Lost in Space: Living Forever, Creating Environmental Sustainability, and Crowd-Funding Lessons from the Space Economy, with Samson Williams
- Space as a Service, Lessons from Space, with Zee Zheng and SpaceChain

Trading and Investing

- Building the next generation alternative investment banking, Paulius Stankevicius
- How to Overcome Depression When Trading and Investing in Cryptocurrencies, with Jay H. Tepley
- Institutional Insights: Bitcoin, Ethereum, Tether, and Altcoin Market Analysis with Mike McGlone
- Pitfalls and Rewards of Options Trading with 100X Leverage and its Impact on India's Crypto Adoption

- Starting from Zero and Challenges with Deep Tech Investing, with Sonny Vu and AREVO
- Tech, security and global crypto growth insights with Samy Karim Binance Smart Chain Ecosystem
- The Shadow CEO, and former poker pro, Athan Slotkin, shares his crypto investing tips for professional and college students new to the cryptosphere.
- VC Investing in Projects with Usability and Sustainability, Rui Zhang, gumi Cryptos Capital

Web 3.0

- Building the Web 3.0 with Deeper Network's decentralized VPNs, with Eric Ma
- Controlling and Sharing your Data with Data Unions, Ethereum maximalist Shiv Malik
- Effectively Transitioning Clients to the Web 3.0 Economy by Doing Public Relations Right and Building the Crypto PR Firm of

the Future, with Kurt Ivy @ Simple Crypto PR
- The Race Against an Orwellian Future is ON, Let's Go!!, with Geoff McCabe @ LetsGo
- What you need to know about Web 3.0 with Jeremy Lindblad and Chibi Dinos
- Why Artists Should Create Their Own Platforms for Fan Engagement, DJ Sam Feldt, Fangage
- Winning the Churn Wars and Creating Lifetime Value through Digital Streaming in the Web 3.0 Economy, with Andrea Berry @ Theta Labs
- What's in the Store Now That the Mass Exodus from Web 2 to Web 3.0 Has Begun? With Eric McHugh @ SHOPX

Appendix C: Crypto Hipster's Chronicles

These are a combination of three to five clips from the Crypto Hipster Podcasts by common theme, thread of topic. A complete list of Jamil's Crypto Hipster's Chronicles is presented below. All of them can be found at anchor.fm/crypto-hipster-podcast and can be listened to on Spotify, Apple Podcasts, Amazon, Anchor, or wherever enjoy your favorite podcasts.

- Episode 1: Unstoppable Authors
- Episode 2: DeFi: Why Wall Street is Running Scared
- Episode 3: Metaverse Metamorphosis
- Episode 4: The Pursuit of Trust and Altruistic Good

- Episode 5: Crypto Gaming Ancients and Heroes
- Episode 6: Lobsters, Apes, Stars and Orangutans
- Episode 7: Hacks, Rugs, and the Court Jester
- Episode 8: NFTs Arising from the Ashes
- Episode 9: Knowledge is Power
- Episode 10: Leveraging Web 3.0 to Build Fan Engagement
- Episode 11: Overcoming Adversity and Building Resiliency through NFTs
- Episode 12: Ukraine: A State in a Smartphone
- Episode 13: Travelling Through Space and Time
- Episode 14: Research, Development, and Production in Crypto-Gaming and the Metaverse
- Episode 15: Early Web 3 and NFT Marketplaces

- Episode 16: Going Above and Beyond to Create a World of Heroes
- Episode 17: Addressing Compliance and Global Regulatory Standards
- Episode 18: Achieving Global Sustainability Goals through Bitcoin Mining and Community Coins
- Episode 19: Early Crypto Trends and Predictions for 2022
- Episode 20: Controlling and Securing Your Personal Web 3 Data and Online Identity
- Episode 21: Breaking: Wall Street!! Why?: Bitcoin
- Episode 22: Crypto Valley Insights: How Switzerland is Poised to Become the Global Crypto Leader
- Episode 23: The Three Musketeers of DAOs (Decentralized Autonomous Organizations) – Governance, Intelligence, and Justice
- Episode 24: How Crypto is Solving the Carbon Neutrality Crisis

- Episode 25: Bitcoin: Are We Achieving Satoshi's Vision?
- Episode 26: Crypto 101: Building a Resiliency Skillset
- Episode 27: War Games, Altruism, and Blockchain for Peace
- Episode 28: DEFI-ing the Future of Finance for Retail and Institutional Crypto Adoption
- Episode 29: Uplifting Creators and Collectors through Cutting-Edge Technologies and Innovation (featuring Tree Trunk)
- Episode 30: Ethics, Conviction, and Resiliency – Important Personal Traits or Blockchain Cornerstones?
- Episode 31: Funds, Crypto Banks, and Direct Investments – Doing DeFi in Different Ways
- Episode 32: Building Equitable Futures and Healthy Ecosystems with Crypto Tokens, NFTs, and Metaverses

- Episode 33: Discovering Your Inner NFT in the Real World and the Metaverse
- Episode 34: Crypto Hipster Podcast's Submission to Irish Podcast Awards for Podcast of the Year
- Episode 35: A Critical Look For Us Beyond Just Web 3.0
- Episode 36: Starting from Zero: How to Build a Powerful Personal Blueprint for Success
- Episode 37: Helping Online Publishers Build Bright and Abundant Futures
- Episode 38: The Pitfalls and Rewards of Crypto Trading and Investing
- Episode 39: Malware, Gem Wear, and Underwear: Measuring Blockchain's Beneficial Impact on Disparate Industries
- Episode 40: Land Grab! Empowering Real Estate Owners and Healthcare Participants in the Web 3.0 Economy

- Episode 41: Crypto Across the 4 Corners: Blockchain and Bitcoin Insights from Around the World
- Episode 42: Creating a Path Forward in Decentralized Finance for Global Banks and Institutions
- Episode 43: The Strength of the Triangle Mindset: Leveraging the Intersection of Artificial Intelligence, Machine Learning and Blockchain Technology to Benefit Humanity
- Episode 44: Why Economists and Environmentalists Are Often WRONG About Bitcoin
- Episode 45: The Digital Crypto Future is Coming Sooner Than You Think

www.ingramcontent.com/pod-product-compliance
Lightning Source LLC
Chambersburg PA
CBHW071410210526
45465CB00001B/328